The Rise from Pain to Passion

Ethel Tippit

The Rise from Pain to Passion

Copyright © 2019

Publication date: April 7, 2019

ISBN: 9781090306548
LCCN: 2019937459

Cover design image: by Phyllis Clemmons
Interior layout: by Phyllis Clemmons
Logo image: by Scott Baker
E-mail: etheltippit@gmail.com
Cellular phone #210 237-2362
Website: www.paintopassion.com

FOREWORD

This is a story of child molestation and sexual abuse that was encountered by a young girl between the ages of 3 and 11 years old.

Her name is Ebony Eloquent Richards. This story is based on the abuse she experienced, an exploitation that left her bitter for many years to come.

After Ebony gave her heart and her life to the Lord, she realized that her feelings of guilt and shame for the mistreatment she had to endure were unfounded. The enemy had planted a seed of deception in her young mind, causing Ebony to believe that somehow, she must have been at fault.

Since her salvation, the Spirit of the Lord has imparted revelation within her. She now understands that the responsibility of her past does not rest upon her. She is only accountable for her future. Because of her restoration, she can now tell her story without feelings of disgrace and without worry or regard for what some folks may say. Ebony knows that God has promised to uphold her with his righteous right hand. His word says, "Fear not, for I am with you; be not dismayed, for I am your God; I will strengthen you, I will help you, I will uphold you with my righteous right hand." Isaiah 41:10 (ESV)

Her prayer for you all, is that this story inspires you to embrace God's healing hand. Therefore, as you read about Ebony's journey from pain to passion, know that it is possible for you also.

Phyllis Clemmons

ACKNOWLEDGEMENT

I would like to thank my spiritual mother, Apostle Phyllis Terry, who has inspired me to be all that God wants me to be, including an author and a writer.

I would also like to thank my spiritual father, Thomas Terry, whose belief in me also inspired me to write this book. You will always be "Dad" to me.

Last, but definitely not least, I would like to thank my children for hanging in there and not giving up on me.

There were times when I wanted to give up, but I thank God that he not only saved me, but he saved the three of you as well! I love you Michael T, Ashley L. and Shanese N…HATS OFF TO YOU ALL.

DEDICATION

This book is dedicated to my mother and father. God bless their soul. RIP Mom and Dad.

PREFACE

This book is based on a true story. The actual names have been changed to protect the innocent. It gives accounts of abuse that Ebony suffered at the hands of a medical doctor at an extremely young age.

The story is written to help others who have experienced similar trauma, to heal from the wounds caused by childhood molestation. It is a type of molestation that often occurs with those who are familiar to the victim. It is often a relative, a close family friend, a priest, and yes, even the family doctor. This story demonstrates that abuse of this kind does not discriminate. It reaches the rich and famous, the poor and unknown, the good, the bad and the ugly. It crosses gender and cultural lines and violates the very young and even the very old.

It started for Ebony at the tender toddler stage of 3 years old. How could this happen you ask? She was just a baby. Surprisingly, many are beginning to speak out, boldly announcing, "Me too!" Finally, a bright light is shining on deep secrets that have been hidden and swept under the rug for many years, secrets that many were warned not to expose, secrets that caused those who were victimized much emotional trauma, mental anguish, and pain.

Behold! It is a new day, a new time, a season of revelation. Sexual predators who thought they had escaped justice, their sins are finally being uncovered. Some whose indiscretions happened many years ago are now being exposed.

Those who have not been discovered and brought to justice will not escape the wrath of God. Your deeds will not go unpunished!

Be not deceived; God is not mocked: for whatsoever a man soweth, that shall he also reap. Galatians 6:7 (KJV).

CHAPTER 1

IN THE BEGINNING

Ebony was born on a cold, winter day. The holiday season had just ended.

Being poor, the holidays were generally not a good time of the year, (or so she was told).

It didn't help that her mother was pregnant with her and unknowingly, her twin brother. They were both delivered in January of 1963.

"Push! Push! It's a girl! But wait, her mother was still having strong contractions after the baby was born. She didn't have to push again, something was happening. She felt something more. It seemed to be thrusting hard against the vaginal opening. Something else was pushing its way out. Was it the placental expulsion? No, it was another baby, a boy! Everyone was shocked. Ebony's mother hadn't known she was pregnant with twins. The sonogram only showed one baby.

The doctor said sometimes the second baby is hidden behind the first, the rhythm of their heartbeats in sync with one another. In such cases, it's impossible to detect the presence of another child. Her parents were unprepared for twins.

Having twins was not the greatest thing that could have happened to a poor family, especially when twins were not expected. At the time, Ebony's mother was in her 40's and her dad was in his late 50's. Nevertheless, both mother and father embraced the twins' entry into the world.

Ebony's mother would always tell people when the twins were born, everyone thought Ivan was the girl and Ebony was the boy as her brother had a head full of hair, but Ebony, on the other hand was born almost bald. Why she felt the need to share that with friends and family on a regular basis, Ebony did not know!

Ivan also looked a lot younger than her. Probably because he was so tiny at birth. They did not know if he would make it. They said she took all the nutrition from him in the womb. Actually, she went home after two days while Ivan remained in the hospital for another month, because he was so small, which is why people assumed she was the oldest all the time.

This time, MD would serve as the family obstetrician for the last time. The family was complete. But he was still the doctor known as their "family doctor." He was the one her mother called on for everything and anything.

Three years later, when Ebony's aunt got sick, MD was summoned. When she died, he was there. You see, her mom had two sisters. One lived with them and one lived alone.

Shortly after Ebony's aunt died, MD was the one Ebony's mother called on to serve as the family pediatrician.

She remembers the first time the doctor came to the house. That day marked the beginning of her long and traumatic interactions with MD.

You see, he was known as the good family doctor everyone knew and trusted. He also had a reputation for doing these, so called "good deeds," which made him known throughout the community by everyone. But unknown to the world, there was a terrible secret. It was a secret no one ever talked about or acknowledged, not back then, not ever.

The so called "good deeds" he gave to her family were not free. They came at a price. Ebony had been chosen as the sacrifice. The one designated to pay that price!

Ebony Richards is her name and this is her story.

CHAPTER 2

EBONY

Ebony remembers her life growing up, as far back as 3 years old. They lived in a small town in Louisiana in an old wooden house that badly needed painting. It had an attic and a large kitchen and living room. She doesn't remember exactly how many bedrooms it had, but she remembers sleeping in her parent's room.

They could not afford a house big enough for everyone to have their own room. You see, the occupants of that old house were: her parents, Rosa and Amos Richards. Two brothers, Ivan and Malek, one sister, Misty and her aunt, Sharon. Her twin brother Ivan and her older brother, Malek shared the attic. Her sister, Misty and her Aunt Sharon shared a bedroom. Times were hard back then for Ebony's family. They didn't have a lot, but they had what they needed and they had each other.

Ebony also had another sister named Penny and another brother named Edward, who was killed in a fire before she and Ivan were born. They did not grow up with her and her other siblings. They were the products of Ebony's father's previous union with his former wife. All Ebony knew was that her brother, Edward, his wife and their three young children were intentionally burned to death in their home. This left her dad devastated. But because he knew God, he was able to get through it and move on. This situation was instrumental in bringing Ebony to an awareness of God. But in time, her experiences would cause her to come to know God as "Lord and Savior."

Her dad was a farmer at that time. He had chickens, pigs, and hunting dogs, which explains why they always had chicken and pork to eat. They also would have other meats whenever her dad went hunting and brought back his kill. He also went fishing a lot, so they ate fish a lot. As a result, Ebony hates fish.

Ebony remembered thinking how some of the animals her dad hunted looked funny to her, especially the coons and rabbits. But at least they didn't go hungry. Other than hunting, her dad also left for work early in the morning with a lunch box and came home late in the evening. Her mother was a stay at home mom. She took care of the house. She also took care of her sister, Sharon when she became ill, in addition to taking care of Ebony and her siblings.

Her parents didn't have much education, so the jobs her dad was able to get were manual labor and payed little. Her dad had to quit school in the 6th grade and her mom quit school in the 3rd grade. It was not by choice.

They were share croppers growing up and had to work in the fields. Ebony could not say for sure, but she sensed that her mom had some type of mental disability. Things of that nature were never discussed back then and they were rarely diagnosed.

At any rate, her mom did not work for many years. So, her father's contribution was their only income. She surmises this is the reason they had very little in the way of toys growing up.

She and her twin brother used to literally share toys. They would get one bike or one wagon or one whatever for Christmas and sometimes even for birthdays. Sometimes they got nothing for their birthday because it came in early January, right on the heels of Christmas. But they always got their own cake! Ivan liked chocolate and Ebony's favorite was peanut butter cake. Her mom made the best peanut butter cakes on this side of heaven! It was very special to Ebony.

Even though there were hard times, Ebony remembers a lot of fun times in that house with her siblings also. Even though her older brother, Malek, was eight years older than she was, he still did a lot with Ivan and Ebony. They had only a few store bought toys, so Malek would make things for them like playhouses, wooden scooters and wagons. He even built them a swing set!

Although he was kind of goofy, he made sure they did not feel the sting of being poor. As a matter of fact, Ebony was unaware of anything lacking in their financial situation. She was only able to discern they had less than some of their other friends when she became much older.

In that old house, Ebony also remembers a very bad time. Her aunt Sharon got sick and died in that old house. She didn't know if her aunt ever went to the doctor. She only knew that a doctor used to come to their house. The day her aunt Sharon passed away, Ebony recalls being very scared. She didn't quite understand what was going on. She just remembers observing her mother and her mother's sister, aunt Clara, was crying a lot.

Aunt Clara was the aunt that did not live with them, she just came around a lot. She was Ebony's favorite aunt. She'd never seen Aunt Clara cry before. But that day, she was crying uncontrollably. It was at this time that MD, the family doctor, began to act differently towards her family, (or so it seemed in her young eyes). Ever since Ebony could remember, the good doctor seemed to always be around.

It was odd, because it was almost unheard of back then, that a poor black family would even have a family doctor.

So, it seemed unnatural for him to be there at her aunt's passing. In addition, he was acting weird. Ebony recalls being outside and hearing loud voices coming from inside of the house. She ran to the front door and when she opened the door, she saw the good doctor choking her Aunt Clara. Everyone in the house came flying out of the door. That left Ebony in a state of shock! She thought he was trying to kill her!! But perhaps he was just trying to calm her down. Nevertheless, it scared her badly! Ebony never told anyone what she thought she'd seen. In those days, you were strictly forbidden to talk about family business outside of the house. Whatever went on in the house, stayed in the house.

After that day, MD looked big and scary to her. On the other hand, although Ebony was only three years old, she must have looked good to him. After that day, the weirdness never went away. After that day, Ebony seemed to be the target of the good doctor's affections, causing her to cringe from the memory of every single encounter she had with him.

CHAPTER 3

THE GOOD DOCTOR

Ebony was born with asthma. She was on medication for that condition for years. As far back as she could remember, she was treated by MD for her asthma.

Her mother thought that he was okay as she trusted him to the point of blind obedience. Ebony's mother was uneducated and this made it difficult for her to find work. It occurred to her that MD may have been taking advantage of her also. Especially when they were a single income household with many mouths to feed.

He may have even been paying her to let him have his way with Ebony. Otherwise, it was hard for her to believe that her mother would knowingly allow such abuse to go on without doing something about it.

MD was very slick. He would request to see Ebony at least once a month and her mother complied with his wishes. Because of their financial status as a low income family, he may have been giving her money to help make ends meet. Although he did not specify why he gave her the money, Ebony felt it must have been the tactic he deliberately arranged to get her mother to continue bringing her to see him. The bottom line is, she didn't have much of a choice anyway. He was the only physician in their little town and he helped them when they needed it. He always gave Ebony money whenever she went to see him.

It seemed like after her aunt died, he saw Ebony much more than he saw her twin brother, Ivan. Even though Ivan was half her size at birth and stayed in the hospital a month longer than she did, he rarely went to the doctor that Ebony was made aware of.

She now believes in some sick, sadistic way, he thought giving her money kept him from feeling guilty about his actions. His so called "help," came at a price. It was a price that Ebony was forced to pay not once or twice, but for many, many years, causing bitterness towards her mother.

For some reason, he was able to always have a smile on his face in spite of his offensive actions towards Ebony.

The only time she recalls seeing him upset was the time he came to the house when her aunt Sharon died and Ebony thought he was choking her aunt Clara. She also remembers that there were a couple of times when either she or Ivan had gotten hurt, and he refused to see them.

Her mom would say he was either high or drunk when he would not come to the door of his office. She seemed to have permission to visit his office anytime of the day or night. This may be because his office served as a mini emergency room.

There were always people in the waiting room no matter what time of the day or night they went. Sometimes, he would lock the doors, preventing patients from entering. Nevertheless, a lot of people liked him simply because he gave to the poor on a regular basis. Not only did he give money, he often gave free medical treatment.

Sometimes when he came to Ebony's house, he would even hang around drinking with her dad. He would even go so far as to give her older brother, Malek, the keys to his sports car.

Ebony often wondered if he treated his white patients the same way he did her family and other black families or not. Although she believe he actually was a help to the black community in some ways, she wondered if there was an unspoken motive, as she could see the difference in his method of operation used between the two cultures.

For example, his office had two entrances. One entrance was for whites and one entrance was for blacks. There were nice sofas and chairs in the waiting room that was set aside for MD's white patients. However, the waiting room for his black patients had folding chairs.

She assumed that was why he could mistreat little girls and their mothers, who were less fortunate, and get away with it. Reporting incidents of molestation back in those days were unheard of. That is why we have such a big "Me too" movement going on now. There was one important fact that Ebony would discover because people were brave enough to come forward and expose so called prominent people. She found out that abuse was not limited to a color or gender of people. She found out it could, and has happened to people of all cultures.

During the time Ebony was growing up, she wanted desperately to tell someone, but she didn't know who she could tell, as her mother was present during some of her doctor's appointments with MD, yet she never said a word. Ebony thought if she did not do anything to defend her daughter, she must approve of what he was doing. This fact was confusing to her as her instincts led her to believe that something was not right with it, but because there was no objection from her mother, she believed it was normal. She believed that all children were 'examined' in this manner every month. Every time Ebony was taken to see MD, there were always lots of mothers with their little girls in the waiting room. As she thought back on it years later, she would often wonder if he molested them all, at one time or another.

Ebony was never able to understand why her twin brother Ivan, who was always sick, was not taken to see the doctor nearly as much as she was. As she mentioned previously, Ivan was born anemic and spent the first month of his life in the hospital. Maybe he went at a different time from Ebony. She is not absolutely sure as her and Ivan have never talked about it to this day.

Her mother did not drive so they would always walk to his office during the time when Ebony's father was at work. She is not sure where her other siblings were but assumes they may have been at school because they never came with them to the doctor's office.

Upon arrival at the doctor's office, Ebony would be escorted inside the door for the black patients and had to wait to be seen. When it was her turn, the nurse would appear at the door and call Ebony's name. She would smile and take her hand, leading her to the end of a long, dark corridor to an examination room where MD would be waiting. He would tell her to undress and he would leave the room. Sometimes the nurse would leave and come back shortly after Ebony had disrobed, and most of the time she stayed with Ebony.

He would proceed to go through his routine, which consisted of using his fingers to touch her all over. There were areas that his hands lingered in for extended periods of time. Even at such a young age, there was something about his touching that struck her as inappropriate. Along with the pain, she felt embarrassed and ashamed, although she was not quite sure why, as the nurse was always there, looking on and continuing to smile while the doctor did his 'examination.'

When he was finished he would instruct her to get dressed and as usual, he would give her $5 or $10. Afterward, the nurse would take her back to the waiting room. Ebony's mother never discussed anything pertaining to what went on during these visits.

The strangest thing would happen sometimes during these visits. Before they left his office to return home, Ebony's mother would go in the back where MD was. She would have a bag with a butter container or something similar with her to give to MD while she was in the examining room. However, when she came out, she was empty handed.

Ebony does not know to this very day, if butter was in the container, or something else, as she was not permitted to go in the back on those occasions. She had to wait in the waiting room until her mother returned.

When Ebony thought of it years later, she wondered if the doctor had been doing inappropriate things with her mother as well.

Whatever went on, when her mother was in the back alone with MD, her mother would take that secret to her grave.

It was common in those days that grownups did not engage in conversations with children regarding such matters. They always walked home from the doctor's office, quickly and quietly. Sometimes her dad would be home sleeping on the couch when they got back. He never asked her what went on at the doctor's office and Ebony never told him.

Her mind would always come back to certain questions, *were other little girls having the same experiences she'd had at the hands of the good doctor?*

For years she'd wanted to ask girlfriends she'd grown up with, but she was afraid and also because it was depicted by the doctor, the nurse, and her mother as something that was hidden and should never be discussed. Through the actions of those who should have protected her, she was led to believe that what happened to her was an everyday normal occurrence for all little girls. Yet, it was deemed unacceptable conversation. It was an act that she wanted to end and for a while, she thought it had. When Ebony was 8, her mother stopped taking her to see MD.

She felt relieved, she didn't ask her any questions about it. She was just happy she didn't have to go anymore. Then one day, her parents took her, for what seemed like a very long car ride. They pulled up to a tall, stately building, then they got out of the car and walked inside.

Once again, Ebony noticed there was a familiar atmosphere. They were directed to the right side of the hallway. But the white people who came in were led to the left side of the hallway. Somehow, many of their faces seemed familiar to her, *but it couldn't be,* she thought. Her mother never said a word regarding why they were there. As a matter of fact, there were lots of little girls there with their parents. There were boys too, but mostly girls.

When she asked her why they were there, her mother said MD had a new office. The other one was closed. She didn't know what to expect. This building looked nothing like the old scary looking building that he had when his practice was in their town. He only had one nurse in the other building. This one had a lot of nurses. They also had administrative assistants at windows checking patients in. There were lots of examining rooms in this place.

Everything was so different here, Ebony thought the doctor would be different too. In addition, she did not get called last! She was led to one of the examining rooms by a nice nurse. Although this place was much better than the doctor's office had been in the town where she lived, she was still apprehensive and scared. Then suddenly the door opened, when she looked up, to her surprise, there stood MD, looming larger than she had remembered, he stood right in front of her.

He looked at her with that hungry look, just as he use to have in his eyes. With a big smile on his face he said, "Undress and I will be right back!"

Ebony's heart sank. She started to cry and told MD she did not want to undress. He continued smiling and walked out of the room.

When he came back in, he said to her, "I haven't seen you in a good while, let me see how you are developing." He wanted to put her at ease and so he told her that her mother was right across the hall and wanted her to cooperate and so, she did.

The visits went back to being once a month again as they had been when his practice was in the same town Ebony lived in.

She hated it! She hated MD! She hated her mother! Most of all she hated herself! She cried, questioning why she had been born just to go through this pain. She searched her mind for the answers. Does this happen to all girls? Why didn't God make her a boy? She just didn't understand!

Ebony didn't have a relationship with God at that young age. She thought God was way up in the sky and did not have time for her. She just felt like a little ugly duckling, who was very confused, not understanding why she felt that way.

Question after question would haunt her little mind. *"Was my childhood different from other kids? Was it me? Was it my fault that I was being sexually abused?"*

First, she will share her whole story with you, then she will share the severity of her abuse, then you decide.

CHAPTER 4

THE NIGHTMARE VISITS

These were very hard times in Ebony's life. These visits were sick, and at times, even physically painful. They go far beyond what she is able to share without feeling the emotional pain of it all over again. She told you how it began and the routine that went on during her exams with MD. Now, you will get to hear and better understand why she dreaded it so much.

These inappropriate encounters would occur almost every time Ebony went to see MD. If you have ever been a victim of any type of abuse, just know that you are not alone. In fact, there are thousands of little girls and boys who have grown up, scarred from the nightmare of their suffering. Many have buried the horror of it all so deep within, they were left with traumatic stress disorders and schizophrenic behavior patterns. To this day, the root cause of their mental disorders have never been identified.

In the beginning, his unsuitable behavior began with him just kissing Ebony in the mouth from time to time. It started out that way when she was 3 years old and lasted until she was 4. As time progressed, so did his sexual behavior patterns. He would take her little hand and put it on his private area. When he first began doing that, he would have his clothes on and she would only be required to touch him through his pants. After a while, he began to unzip his pants and put her hand inside of his pants.

She was instructed to keep her hand on his bare flesh throughout the examination. During the examination, he would squeeze her developing breasts. This was preceded by a vaginal and anal exam, while the nurse looked on.

Although Ebony's mother was not always in the room, she was in the room on a few of these occasions. The times that stuck out more acutely in her mind were times when she was stretched out on the examining table. The nurse was on one side of the table and her mother sat in a chair by the door. MD stood at the examining table with his back to her mother. Being a large man, she was unable to see what he was doing and never made a move to position herself in order to fully grasp exactly what was happening right under her very nose.

For years Ebony was taunted by knowing her mother was in the room at times during these exams and never spoke a word or intervened on her behalf. This led her to believe, what she was experiencing must be perfectly normal. After all, she rationed, what mother would stand by and see her child misused in this way?

In later years as an adult, Ebony questioned her mother about these sexual encounters. However, she denied knowing or ever being in the examining room with her during MD's sexual attacks on her young body.

By the time she was 5 years old, his distasteful behavior had further advanced to taking his pants off completely, totally exposing the lower half of his body. Sometimes he would even lay next to her on the table. After his normal routine, he would place his mouth between her legs and afterward he would force Ebony to do the same to him. She hated it all! She also hated the fact that the nurse, (whom she later understood her to be his unwilling accomplice, watched as he violated her little body).

Even though, most of the time MD liked seeing her last, sometimes she was summoned from the waiting room to be "examined" before everyone else was seen.

The nurse, whose name was Miss K, would come and get Ebony and take her upstairs to an attic. There she would wait until MD came up. Sometimes, it seemed like hours would pass before he came up the attic stairs. She didn't mind though, as Ebony would climb up in Miss K's lap while she read to her, until she fell asleep.

Sometimes she would sit on the floor opposite Ebony watching her as she played with a box of toys. She would always look at Ebony with a smile on her face. She never said much to her or to MD in Ebony's presence.

During his abuse, Miss K never attempted to stop him. This was another reason why she thought the abuse must be normal, as the two people Ebony trusted allowed her to be violated and never did anything to stop it. She would surmise later that he must have had something he held over their heads to keep them quiet and complacent as he performed these horrible acts.

One day when Miss K and Ebony were upstairs in the attic, she fell asleep and MD came up to carry her down the stairs. She awoke just as he lifted her from Miss K's lap. After they reached the examining room, he sat her on the table and told her to undress. Ebony began to cry as she thought she was about to go home based on the amount of time she had been there. She wanted her mom. Where was she? This day would turn out to be the worse day of her childhood!!

MD undressed himself from the waist down. After his usual exam of Ebony's breast, vaginal and anal areas, he began to handle her roughly as he ravaged her little body. She tried to make eye contact with Miss K to signal her for help, but she had her head down. Ebony was scared, she had no one to help her. She started to cry as he was much rougher than usual. Something was different. Something was wrong.

Ebony tried to resist him, she wanted to get dressed but he said she was getting to be a big girl. She felt so afraid having to endure this atrocity. His wet mouth performing as a vacuum in places her instincts perceived it should not have been. That day he was doing "extra," doing more disgusting acts than he normally did for a longer period of time then he ever had in the past. She thought it was never going to end. After what seemed like forever, he was finished. He walked over to his chair and sat down. He started laughing and telling her how she was a big girl now. He finally allowed her to get dressed. After Ebony was dressed, he reached in his wallet and handed her a $10 bill. She would never forget that day!

It was that day, Ebony started to disappear inside. The visits got more disturbing as time went on. Everything you could possibly imagine, he did it.

Ebony felt so lost and alone. There was no one she could tell, no one to help her. She didn't know a lot about prayer or what to say. Nevertheless, she would ask for angels to come down from heaven to help her.

Her tears did not stop him. Miss K did not stop him, and Ebony's mother did not, would not, or could not stop him. Even the Angels did not stop him. The only thing she could do was hide within herself.

After that unusually horrific day, whenever he would tell her to undress, she would begin to talk to herself.

She would tell herself, "Don't worry, it won't hurt this time. I will hide you. Becoming two people was the only way she was able to survive.

Whenever she had to sustain the emotional, mental, and physical pain of her abuser, she would go inside of herself. It was as though she was able to split herself into two separate entities. One was the helpless little girl lying on that table and the other was the angelic being who floated above the table, praying for that little girl she looked down on as she was being brutally victimized.

There were times when she would remember going into the back, but her mind would block out everything and she could not even remember if she actually saw him that day or not. She would hear her mother's voice calling to her, but was afraid to ask her, "Did I see the doctor yet?" By this time, she would be sitting on the floor in the waiting room fully dressed.

She hated her life. She hated those monthly visits as they became more and more painful in every aspect and Ebony went deeper and deeper inside of herself. Each visit ending in Ebony crying, coughing and gagging, even to the point of throwing up in the sink. But MD didn't care. He would only smile as he hugged and comforted her after each offensive encounter. Always ending by saying, "You are becoming a big girl now. One day, I will be able to penetrate you and then you will get $20." How humiliating! How degrading! Big girl! She was only 6 years old!!!

Around the time Ebony turned 8 years old, it was not just at his office that she would become two people or black out completely whenever she was in these painful situations. She began experiencing these blackout spells and turning into two people also at home, in school, and also whenever a nightmare would occur. In her mind, she would turn into an angel and fly high above the situation to pray for the helpless little girl she looked down on.

Ebony was an adult before she understood what had happened to her mentally.

To this day, there are still things she has blocked from her memory. When whippings at home got bad, she would black out. When kids bullied her at school, she would pretend to be someone else. She would now always choose to leave her body whenever she didn't want to feel anything. She felt trapped, never as a child divulging what she had been through. Whenever something would happen, she would just go inside of herself, feeling like this is what little kids go through. It made her feel bad for all the kids she knew. Even though she never shared what had happened to her, she felt like it had happened to others as well. However, she never said anything because MD told her it was their little secret.

Parents, please don't allow your kids to feel like telling a bad secret is a bad thing. Ebony shares how disappointed she feels when she hears parents teaching their kids not to be a

snitch or that grownups are always right.
These are lies from the pit of hell!

The worse thing about all of this is she
had nowhere to go to hide from him. She had
no one she could tell. Even if she told, what
would she say? Who would listen? Who
would believe her? Do these questions sound
familiar?

It was the word of a poor little black girl
against the word of a prominent white
physician during the era of the sixties and
seventies. But rest assured, she still has the
scars, as well as the therapy bills, to prove it.

Ebony's life was a very painful nightmare.
From age 3 to 11. She didn't know how to
overcome it. She hated her childhood, she
hated her doctor, she hated herself and yes,
sometimes she still hated her mother. She felt
like her mother abandoned her and didn't
protect her when she needed it most.

Parents, it is your right and your
responsibility to know what goes on with
your children. Talk to them. Let them know

they can come to you with anything. Never just dismiss what they say or accuse them of lying until you check out their accusation for yourself. Often children won't just make up something of that magnitude. Although the visits stopped at age 11, the damage it did remained for many years to come.

They moved to a different town and Ebony just decided one day to tell her mom she was done. She didn't argue. She just said okay, like it was up to Ebony all along! Nevertheless, she could close that chapter in her life forever.

CHAPTER 5

CHILDHOOD MEMORIES

As a child, Ebony had to deal with more than just the sexual abuse. She was not the prettiest or the smartest child in the family. Misty was the prettiest and Malek was the smartest. She was called names in school like: ugly, bald headed, blackie and numerous other derogatory names.

At home, she was made to feel less than the other children as well. Their approach was spoken in a more subtle manner but she was still able to feel the sting of her family's insinuations.

She had short hair and was a bit chunky. She would describe it as being "healthy" by the world's standards. In comparison to her twin brother Ivan, who was small and anemic, she appeared to be big.

Ebony really had no friends in elementary school. To make up for what she lacked in other areas, she excelled academically, knowing that was the one thing no one could take away from her. Ebony was an AB student from 1st grade on, making usually all A's, but occasionally she had one or two B's. She actually felt good when she brought home straight A's on her report cards. That was something special that got her the attention she craved, at least for a little while. Even in school, some kids liked her for her brain. She was sought out for the answers to a test or to let them see her answers. They also wanted her to let them copy her work. She remembers an incident in 3rd grade where she was taunted by a little boy on the playground because she covered her paper during a test when he tapped her on her shoulder for an answer to a question.

Being a straight 'A' student also came with the perk of gaining her mom's approval. Deep down inside, she resented her for not only the abuse, but for not loving her like she believed her mother loved her older brother. He was smart. When he went to college, she bragged on him all the time. That seemed to be the one area Ebony could compete with

Malek, as she always bragged on her as well when she got good grades and Ebony liked that.

No one ever really knew how she really felt. She had to create an outlet for herself. It was to make people laugh.

At an early age she would make up jokes about herself before others had a chance to. She was very comical and was able to do impromptu stand-up comedy at school, at home or anywhere else.

Her strategy was, if she made jokes about herself, others would think it did not bother her very much and they wouldn't do it. She considered herself to be an "ugly duckling" growing up. Her older sister, Misty, was very pretty. She was what people often referred to as "high yellow." Her stature was tall and slim. Only those who knew the family knew that Misty and Ebony were sisters. Otherwise those who didn't know, would not have guessed. But Misty was always quick to take every opportunity to remind her sister and everyone else, that they did not favor in appearance.

Misty was a hair stylist and worked in different shops, including a shop at her home. When Ebony was a teenager, she would visit her sister, who would never fail to tell everyone, "Everybody this is my little sister, Ebony. Do we look alike?" Misty was well aware, they didn't look alike and the constant reminder made Ebony feel uncomfortable in her own skin. However, in all fairness, Ebony never confided her feelings to Misty and so her sister never knew the embarrassment it caused Ebony.

Ebony's self-esteem suffered as she felt her sister was making fun of her all the time. The truth of the matter was, Misty didn't know it bothered her sister at all, as Ebony had developed the skill of telling jokes about herself throughout the years, which placed a barrier within herself in order to protect her true feelings about her perception of inadequacy regarding her appearance.

In later years, Ebony realized that it would probably have been better if she'd just shared her true feelings about the situation. It would have been settled a long time ago and Misty would not have continued doing it.

Eventually, Ebony did talk to her sister about it and Misty shared that she was not trying to make fun of her sister and thought she had pretty skin and Misty admired that attribute as she felt like her skin was not as nice as Ebony's.

She was trying to give her a compliment by comparing their two different skin types. Back in the day Misty had what was known as liver splashes, which looked like freckles.

Although Ebony is not sure if that was the case, what she did know is Misty was her sister and she loved her and made the choice to believe her silly explanation.

On the other hand her older brother, Malek, never called attention to Ebony's looks in that way, although he was very handsome. He didn't have to though, because her mother, openly praised him around his siblings as well as around other people.

She bragged on him being smart and she bragged on him graduating from college. Her parents were both very proud of his accomplishments. Whenever she and Ivan wanted something, they would send Malek to ask for it, as her parents were not in the habit of saying no to Malek's requests.

Her parents always told them "No" and him "Yes." For some reason, they treated him like royalty and the rest of them like servants. Don't get her wrong, they were not abused at home but just treated unequally as it pertained to Malek.

Ebony remembers from a young age, they started calling him the *king*! "We would go through the house saying, bow to the king and we would then bow at his feet." He thought it was cute at first, but after a while he began to feel bad and asked them to stop. He said, "That's not true." Ebony believes he realized it was true and felt uncomfortable with the title as well as them bowing down to him. However, they still maintained a very close relationship with him. At least Malek, Ivan, and Ebony. Her sister hung around with her mom most of the time and didn't like hanging with them very much. She was a girly girl and Ebony was a tomboy. Misty hated getting dirty and thought they were too silly, especially Malek. Imagine that! Kids who liked to play seemed silly to her. In spite of how her sister felt, Ebony loved playing with her brothers. Even though Malek was the oldest, he was always fun to be around and he did crazy things. He was a trickster.

Ebony and Ivan would fall for every trick he played on them, and they would often get into trouble. They always bore the brunt of Malek's pranks, as their parents disliked reprimanding him. No matter what kind of shenanigans he initiated, her and her twin Ivan, would get yelled at for screaming and laughing too loudly, or running through the house, with Malek in hot pursuit.

He brought them so much joy that it was worth the stern warning usually given by her mother. As earlier stated, Malek was 8 years older than them and a real jokester. (He has not changed to this day). Ebony enjoyed being around Malek because he didn't judge her, talk about her, or make her feel bad around his friends. He just loved his little sister. Her twin was the same way.

Ivan was cuter than her, she thought, but he did not make fun of her. At least not more than twins normally do. It didn't matter though, because she was bigger than him and could beat him up if she wanted to, and sometimes, she wanted to. Nevertheless, they were like two peas in a pod growing up. Yes, they had their fights like most siblings. But they never stayed mad at each other for very long. Even to this day, they are still very close. Ebony can sense when something is wrong with his health.

Ebony had to come to the realization that all families have that one that may look or act different, but in her position, it was very painful to feel that she was the one in her own home. She never said anything. She just laughed at the joke's others made, her family made, and she herself made. It was easier than dealing with it. To this day, her family does not know her whole story. Some, even after reading this book, still won't believe her.

As an adult looking back, Ebony has become more aware of the feelings of children. "It is easy for us to tell our children to blow it off when something happens, or to tell them it is okay, they'll be all right." But the truth is, some children are more sensitive than others. For the child who is going through abuse, a school fight could traumatize them. People used to think because Ebony was able to joke about the way she was, she must be okay with it. Yet, every day she was dying on the inside. She flinched at the thought of an unkind word. She kept wondering from day to day what would happen at school. One day, as a group of girls stared and headed in her direction, the sound of drums in her ears got louder and louder before she realized it was her heart pounding against her chest. Why were they looking at her? She could feel the cool tingly feeling of sweat running down her face as fear gripped her. Was this the same girls who pushed her into a puddle of mud? Or the ones that snatched a jacket from the clutches of her fingers on a cold day. Her ears began to ring with a loud penetrating sound that seemed deafening as she contemplated if she should run. As they got closer, she could barely hear their loud laughter over the ringing in her ears.

What were they up to? "Ebony! Ebony," one of the girls cried out. "Ebony! Come on, the bell is ringing!" *The bell,* Ebony thought. Whew! It was the school bell. Recess was over. She'd made it through her vain imagination unscathed.

Ebony had a friend whose daughter was a bit chubby growing up, her nickname was "Miss Piggy" or sometimes her friend called her "fatty." Ebony would tell her friend that offensive name calling was not very nice.

She would tell her that her daughter likes it and she dances around and laughs when she is called by those names. Ebony tried to explain to them, based on her own childhood experiences, that she may not like it as much as she pretends. But as a seven-year-old, how else can she act? Her friend also told Ebony that she's concerned that in the future she may be overweight because she does eat a lot, even when she is not hungry.

Ebony reminded her friend, unbecoming name calling tends to invoke the behavior that is characteristic of the name. Ebony asked her, "Do you realize what pigs are known for? Names mean something." Pigs are omnivores, they eat almost anything edible, both plants and other animals. When you speak over her with names like, 'Miss Piggy,' or 'fatty,' you cause her to react as a pig would, by eating everything in sight." They did not understand the predicament that child was in or the ramifications of the names spoken over her. Today, she is in her 20's and weighs over 200 lbs. This does not surprise Ebony as unfavorable names were also spoken over her from a young age.

It is Ebony's wish to encourage parents to choose their words wisely. Remembering that kids become what you call them. She is not saying that all kids are effected the same way. But, she is speaking from a place of knowing the power of words and how the atmosphere can cause the earth to respond to the words that have been continuously verbalized over someone's life.

Ebony hopes her personal childhood experiences will help parents understand the reasons for certain behavior. Also, she know that as children grow, they change. All changes do not mean that something is going on. Nevertheless, she encourages parents to talk to their children.

If you find yourself saying "What's gotten into you lately?" Take the time to talk to that child and find out what has gotten into them. Then, listen to what they tell you.

Ebony used to ask her mother questions during her years of abuse. Like, "Why do I have to go to the doctor all the time? I'm not sick anymore. Why do I have to always undress? Why don't you always come in the examining room with me? Why don't you say anything when you do come in?" She would tell her mother she was tired of going to him and didn't want to see him anymore.

Repeating often, how her twin, Ivan, who was always sick, never had to go to the doctor for regular check-ups like she did. She never really had a good answer for Ebony.

Ebony didn't know how long it would have gone on if her and her family had not moved to a different town when she was 11.

She just remembers telling her mother she was fine, and did not want to go back to him as long as she lived. Finally, her mother said, "O.K." She never had to go back to MD again. It was over…or was it? Although that was the end of the doctor examinations and visits, it would be the beginning of her downward spiral.

After they moved in 1974, Ebony never had to see him again as a patient. But unknown to her, the shock she faced all of those years would be replaced by alcohol, drugs, and promiscuity.

CHAPTER 6

PAINFUL RESULTS

Ebony found herself in a very bad place at age 30.

Her downward spiral began at the age of 12 shortly after the family moved to another city. She began to sneak and drink on the weekends with her cousins. They would get together on Saturdays and buy a bottle of MD 2020, Boones Farm or some other kind of wine. They would put their money together and get one bottle and share it. However, it wasn't long before the sharing stopped.

Ebony rationalized that the wine numbed the pain she was feeling, so having a whole bottle to herself would numb her quickly and it would last twice as long. These were both cheap wines that she managed to buy without someone else having to chip in with her. It was only 75 cents a bottle!

She felt like drinking took her to another place where there was no pain, only fun and freedom to be herself. Little did she know, it would be the beginning of another kind of bondage.

By the time she reached age 14, not only was she drinking wine, but she had also added beer to her drinks of choice. She would get together with like-minded friends and they would have drinking contests to see who could guzzle down 16 ounce cans of Old English 800 the quickest. To Ebony, it was a welcomed event. One that she didn't mind at all. To her it represented a time when she was just having fun.

One day, she and her cousin Charlotte were hanging out near the liquor store and a friend of Charlotte's walked by. She introduced him to Ebony and the two of them struck up a conversation. At that time Ebony was 14 (although she could easily pass for 16) and he was 17. His name was Ray Monroe. He was very cute and it surprised Ebony that he took the time to talk with her. Ray was a senior in high school and Ebony was only in 8th grade. She had talked to a few boys before, but nothing seriously. They were just boys who wanted to fool around in the back seat of a car, but because of her history with the good doctor, she was afraid to.

But Ray was different. He joked around but never got out of line with her or her cousin, at least not right away. He had a friend that lived across the street from Charlotte and they all would play basketball on the week-ends. He would flirt with them about braiding his hair but nothing out of line. He didn't try to force himself on either of them in a sexual way. He was very respectful compared to other boys Ebony had known. She thought that was weird because he was older than the other boys. She wondered why he didn't try to act inappropriately with either of them, largely due to her distorted thinking that all boys must secretly want something from little girls.

She remembers, once a boy asked her to go to his prom as a friend. Ebony was talking to Ray at that time but didn't think he was serious about her. He was one of those cute, high yellow boys that no one thought would talk to her (and neither did she).

Ebony decided to accept his invitation to the prom. The night of the prom, he picked her up but drove past the school to a secluded area. Ebony got scared and asked if they were in fact going to the prom and he said, "After we take care of something else."

She told him she didn't want to. After he tried and begged her, she would only consent to a kiss from him. He got mad and drove her to the neighborhood where he lived and told her to get out. He refused to take her home. It was dark and she was scared, but he insisted.

Ebony exited the car and walked to a cousin's house that did not live too far. She knocked on the door but no one answered. She didn't know what to do. Ebony couldn't believe this was really happening to her. She was too embarrassed to go to anyone else's door, so she just sat down on her cousin's steps and cried for a while.

It would only take Ebony about 20 minutes to walk home, but it was dark. Ever since her aunt died when she was 3, she has been afraid of the dark. So, she sat there, shivering. Fear gripped her. She began to hear all kinds of sounds in the distance. The silence was deafening. Should she make a run for it? Should she wait? Was he coming back? Maybe he was just around the corner. Ebony realized she had to make a decision to move but she would have to pass the town graveyard. That's what really scared her to death! (No pun intended).

Finally, she got up enough nerve to get up and run home. She found out the next day that he went to the prom with another girl. Later she was told, the other girl was his girlfriend.

The events that took place the night of the prom, reinforced her belief that she was ugly and unwanted, just a thing to be used and played with. From that moment on, she decided that she would play them, before they played her.

After that incident occurred, Ebony's second personality became very naughty, so to speak. Not in a sexual way, but very flirty. She vowed not to trust anyone ever again! She never told anyone about what happened the night of the prom, especially Ray. She felt worthless, unloved, ugly, depressed, and lonely.

Nevertheless, Ebony and Ray were getting to be close and she didn't want that to change, even though she didn't think anything serious would come of their relationship. So she continued to keep her guard up. She vowed she would not get hurt again. She figured he was no different from any other boy and would throw her aside once he got what he wanted.

A few months later, Ray graduated from high school and moved to Houston, TX. They continued to talk on the phone as well as write to each other. There were no cell phones back then, so texting was not an option. That summer, Ray asked Ebony if she would be his girlfriend. It was 1977. She said, "Yes."

Ebony felt a sense of excitement. When the summer ended Ray called her said he had decided to join the military! The military! Where they were from, people who joined the military, or left that little town for any reason, never came back! Ray tried to convince Ebony that he was different. Yet, still in the back of her mind, she didn't believe him. Secretly, she thought she would never see him again. Ebony was sad. She remembered thinking to herself, *I should have known.* So, she began to drink heavily and flirt with whoever she wanted to. Besides, her relationship with Ray could never work out as his cousins didn't like her anyway. They thought Ebony was too dark for him, and they told him so.

Everyone laughed when Ebony told them her and Ray were dating. "Not Ray Monroe! He can have any girl he wants. Why would he pick you?" She ignored their negative comments. But once he joined the military, she figured that would be the end of their relationship. In an attempt to block out the emotional pain of losing Ray, she began to drink even more.

By the time she turned 15, Ebony had begun a journey that had no destination. It was a self-medicating journey. It was a painful journey. It was a difficult journey. It was a journey that would lead to alcoholism, drug abuse, and eventually attempted suicide. She drank almost every day. She also began skipping school and hanging out.

No one knew she had a problem. She didn't even know she had a problem.

Somehow she was able to keep her grades up and graduated salutatorian of her 8th grade class. She did what was expected of her at home and sadly, no one noticed her life was being lived from a position of pain. Nobody noticed. Nobody! Nobody seemed to care. Nobody! Ebony wondered, *where was God?*

After graduating from elementary school and going to the 9th grade, she continued to be the class clown. She continued to be funny at home also. No one knew how depressed Ebony really was. They all thought she was really funny and should be a comedian. They would have never guessed that Ebony was not happy. On the contrary, she was very sad.

It wasn't long before Ebony was drinking alone when her friends weren't available. She didn't have a lot of friends anyway. She had cousins, acquaintances, family and the neighbor's kids, but no real friends, except Allison and Dorothy. Allison was her best friend and still is today. Ebony and Allison were friends first, then she met Dorothy.

Ebony, Dorothy and Allison were so close, they were labeled "The Three Musketeers" in high school. They had to stop skipping school so much because if one of the girls was out, the teachers figured they were together.

Despite all this "fun," Ebony was still depressed. Ray was gone and she had not met anyone else that cared for her enough to develop a serious relationship since he left. She continued to "have fun" the only way she knew how, which was to numb the emotional pain she felt, by drinking. Even though Ray was in the military and not expected to come back, he did continue to write. At first, their letters ended with "Sincerely, Ray" and "Sincerely, Ebony." Over time, the closure of their letters would change to "Love, Ray" and "Love, Ebony, or "Later Ebony" to "Bye baby." Just like that, through the mail, their relationship blossomed.

Nevertheless, Ebony still did not think she would ever see him again.

CHAPTER 7

RAY RETURNS

The summer of 1977 went by very fast. She continued to party and was a bit out of control. In December of 1977, Ebony got the surprise of her life! Ray called and said he was coming home! He had gotten stationed about an hour away from their hometown in Louisiana.

He said he was going to come and see her before heading to his first duty assignment and then he would be able to visit every week-end. Ebony was shocked, excited, scared, nervous and afraid to see him again. After all, she had been going along with this relationship on paper all year, but living totally opposite from what she portrayed in her letters. She knew Ray was going to find out that she had been drinking heavily, smoking, flirting and leading guys on. Now he was coming back. She didn't know what she was going to do.

The day finally came. Ray was back! Ebony was very nervous about seeing him again. Ray was going to pick her up at school in front of everybody! She didn't know how to feel. Would she look the same to him? Would he look the same to her? She needed a drink! Yes, she would get dressed and hit the liquor store before school. So she hurriedly dressed, called Allison, and headed out the door to meet her at the liquor store. They purchased and downed a bottle of Ripple. Then, calmly, they headed to school. She wasn't sure what time Ray was coming. The day was almost over. Then it happened! As she was heading to her 6th period class, the last class of the day, she passed a window and saw an unfamiliar car in front of the school just sitting there. She walked pass the door of her class and went outside. She froze as her feet hit the pavement, waiting breathlessly to see if that was really him. The door opened and the boy who'd left to go into the military, stepped out of the vehicle as a man. It was Ray! They came together and embraced like never before. Then he began to kiss her right in front of the school! After that moment, they were inseparable.

He and Ebony were together every day. He had planned to stay for about a week. Before he left, they made it official. They agreed they would be exclusive and only see each other.

By this time, Ebony was in the 9th grade and Ray was already living an Air Force life. Needless to say, they struggled to keep the relationship afloat due to the years between them, but they made it.

After a period of time, they finally consummated their relationship by giving their virginity to each other. It was late summer in 1978. Ebony was staying with her sister and brother, Misty and Malek. One day, while they were both at work, she and Ray were hanging out and he began to kiss her. But this time was different. Ray was about to go away for 6 weeks. He had never made sexual advances toward her before this day. They had kissed in the past, but that was it. This time as they kissed, Ray began to touch her in a way that reminded her of MD and she froze. She never told him what was going on. She just suggested they have a drink and continue. After a couple of drinks, Ebony was able to continue, although this first encounter was very painful.

In the spring/summer of 1979, Ebony became pregnant with their first child. She stopped drinking for the sake of her baby. She realized that there was someone else she had to think about other than herself. Besides, the mere smell of alcohol made her stomach churn. Even a Coke commercial would make her feel nauseated. She wasn't able to consume either of these drinks even if she wanted to. She knew God was watching out for her during that time.

Ray and Ebony's son was born in 1980. They were officially parents! Little Ray looked just like big Ray. (Everybody let her know how good that was).

People also felt the need to let her know how shocked they were that little Ray had a head full of hair. (Some things never change).

It was at that point Ray decided he wanted to marry Ebony. Not long after that, he proposed, and she said yes. She was very excited. The wedding was going to take place months after her high school graduation in 1981.

Ebony's dream was to go to college and she did. The college she attended was two hours away, so her mom kept little Ray during the week, and Ebony lived on campus. Every Friday, she would catch the bus to Ray's duty station and together, they would ride home to see Little Ray for the weekend. They continued that routine until they got married and moved in together.

The wedding was scheduled to take place in 1982 during Ebony's freshman year in college. By that time, she was 19 and had reverted back to her old habit of drinking after little Ray was born. Ray didn't seem to mind. He was so nice. Ebony really cared for him a lot. She thought the sun rose and set on him, especially after they were married.

At the wedding, she drank heavily. It had been a while since she'd smoked, but she started smoking again too.

Not long after, at the age of 21, Ebony and Ray had a daughter. Then, at age 25, they had their third child, it was another girl. She felt like they now had the picture-perfect family. People thought they were the perfect couple. They had made it through the rough teen years. It was a marriage made in Heaven. Ray was so handsome and quiet. Most of all, he loved Ebony! She felt like nobody had ever loved her and she was very lucky that he chose her for his wife.

People would often ask, "Girl how did you end up with Ray Monroe? He could have had anybody he wanted."

Before they were married, he even had cousins that tried to set him up with girls not as "dark-skinned" as she was, but he elected to stay with Ebony, a little short-haired dark skinned, ugly country girl that drank.

Even though Ebony had a good husband and three beautiful, healthy children, she still felt the pain from the sexual abuse at the hands of MD. She still had not yet told anyone, not even Ray.

She needed the numbness to function normally. She had become use to the numbness. It kept her from feeling like she was "less than" with everybody.

Doctor MD had no idea what he took from her back then. She could not bring herself to love herself, even though she sought after the love of other people. Ebony was a giver. She was a people pleaser. She thrived on the affirmation of other people. In her eyes, temporary validation was better than no validation.

She supposed whenever things got rough, or Ray said or did something hurtful, Ebony would laugh it off. She didn't want him to leave her or to get mad at her. Of course, whenever she had to cover up her feelings or silence her tongue, it made her even more depressed and made her drink even more.

It was a never ending, vicious cycle, and a roller coaster that she didn't know how to get off or if she even wanted to. Ray was not abusive, but he had a way about him that made Ebony feel inadequate. Her self-esteem was already at an all-time low.

For instance, after her third child was born, Ebony's weight had increased to a size 16. It was at that point that Ray stopped initiating intimate relations with her, and she found herself in the place of initiator all the time. When she asked him why he had not reached out to her, he said because she had gained so much weight it wasn't the same for him anymore. It would be issues of this magnitude that drove her deeper and deeper into misery.

Between the ages of 26 through age 30, Ebony viewed these as the worse years of her life. She had become a full-blown alcoholic. There were times when Ray would complain that she was drinking too much. Although she would slow down for a few days, it wouldn't be long before the heavy drinking would resume, either with friends or alone.

Ray did not drink nor did he want to be around Ebony when she was drinking, so he would avoid going out with her and her friends. Even though she was not saved, the devil had set a trap to eliminate the future God had in store for her. He wanted Ebony dead!

During their tour in North Dakota, the winters were brutal. After 3 years, they decided to request orders to leave. Ray had never been on a remote tour before. This would mean a separation from the family, while he served in another country.

Ray requested a tour to Keflavik, Iceland and his request was granted. He left without Ebony and the children in 1990. The tour was for one year. She decided to go back to Louisiana while Ray was away.

It was at that time, that Ebony became suicidal. One night, while drinking with some family members, she walked outside to be alone. She was sitting on the steps when she began hearing voices in her head. The voices said: "Look at you! You are nobody! Your kids would be better off without you. You should end it. They won't even miss you. They don't even know you are out here. Nobody cares. Nobody loves you! Go ahead, ease your pain. Ease your pain."

Ebony, very inebriated, holding a glass of beer in her hand, slowly stood to her feet. All kinds of feelings were running through her head. Her past, her present, and seemingly, her future were about to collide. The pain was unbearable. She thought, *would death be better?*

Before Ebony was fully aware of her actions, she was walking out into the street in front of a car. Just as she stepped out, she saw a light and heard a siren go off. It caused Ebony to snap back to reality. In front of her was a police car. *Seriously!* She thought. She couldn't even do that right. Of all the luck! Clearly, God was looking out for her.

The officer got out of the patrol car to talk to her. After, she told him she wanted to take her life, he convinced her she was making a big mistake. Although he allowed her to go back inside the house, she noticed he continued to patrol the area 2 to 3 times a day for the next month.

Sometimes he would stop and talk. Sometimes he would wave and keep going. Even though that was the first real attempt she had made to kill herself, it would not be the last.

When Ray's tour in Iceland was over, the family was reunited for his next tour of duty at an airbase in Florida. Things seemed to be good for a while. Then Ray seemed to be losing interest in her again. Ebony was working as manager of a pizza parlor six days a week. In spite of her long hours, she still managed to find time to drink daily.

She was a "functioning alcoholic." To make matters worse, she started taking drugs again. She would take pills to help her to get going in the morning so she could make it to work by 9:00 a.m. Then by 9 p.m. she would be so tired, she would take another pill to help her stay awake until the parlor was closed and all the paperwork was done. By that time, it was midnight.

Once she got home and got settled, she would be wide awake. In order to get some sleep, she would have a few drinks or take a pill that would help her to sleep. Once again, she found herself in a vicious cycle.

Ebony could tell that Ray was beginning to lose interest in her again because he started making fun of her weight again even though she had lost three dress sizes and was down to a size 12. He still showed her no affection. She continued to lose until she was a size 6-8. Other guys noticed Ebony, but Ray was still not impressed. Imagine that!

Ray could always find something wrong with her. Although, he would say it in a nice way or in a joking way, even in a loving way.

Unknown to him, someone out there was paying attention to that "ugly duckling!"

Ebony had reverted back to the old days before her and Ray got married. She had become very promiscuous again. MD had her so messed up, she didn't know her worth. She craved validation. She was thirsty for love and affection. She wanted and needed to be held and told she was beautiful.

She needed that kind of attention, especially at this juncture of her life. Don't get it twisted, aside from Ray's inability to show Ebony any real affection, he was a good provider and a loving father. He just lacked the capability to give her the kind of affection she so deeply longed for. Whenever affection came her way by other means, she would take it.

Being the manager, she had to stay there after the pizza parlor was closed to do paperwork. Rumors had it that the building was haunted. One night while she was finishing the nightly paperwork, there was banging on the iron racks and other little unexplainable noises. She got really scared. She called Ray to come stay with her and he refused. He told Ebony to get one of her employees to stay. But she was not permitted to have other employees stay on the job off the clock. Although he knew that, he didn't care.

There was a customer that had started coming in almost every other day. His name was Corey Sanders. He would always joke around with her. Corey was about 8 years younger than her. (Ebony didn't know it at the time, as he had previously lied to her about his age). He flirted with her every chance he got. He was very handsome with blond hair and blue eyes.

After trying unsuccessfully to get Ray to come sit with her, she called Corey and asked him to come and stay with her, and he did. When she had completed her paperwork, they decided to go to his place for a drink. One thing lead to another. Shortly thereafter, Ebony found herself in the midst of a full blown affair with him.

She was amazed and excited all at once, someone was interested in her! He liked being around her. She was not too big! She was not too ugly! She was not too dark! She was not too tall. Her hair was not too short! He noticed her! He complimented her! She felt good when she was with him.

Nevertheless, guilt began to overtake her. Ebony drank more so she didn't have to think about it. But when she drank, it made her want to be with him more because he made her feel good. Then the guilt would overwhelm her again and she would become more depressed, so she would drink. So forth and so on. Then the depression got worse from the cycle she had, once again, created for herself.

Then the suicidal thoughts returned. This went on for several years. It had gotten so bad, suicide was not just a thought. It became a viable option in Ebony's mind.

She no longer wanted to live! She had gone too far. She had become unrestrained over the years of being an alcoholic, but still maintained her theory of "playing them before they played her," remember? Only this time Ebony found herself falling in love with Corey.

Not long after, Ebony would have a pregnancy scare. How would she explain a blond haired, blue eyed baby to her husband? Ray had a vasectomy! The devil's plan was unfolding. She wondered if he was about to win.

CHAPTER 8

NO WAY OUT!

On October 22, 1993, Ebony went over to her twin brother's house. It was early in the evening. They both began to drink. She is not able to remember everything they drank that night. Her alcohol problems had reached its peak. They drank, smoked, and took pills too. She did remember leaving her brother's house, but she didn't remember what time it was. She thought it was about 10 p.m., but was later told, it was about midnight.

She remembers dropping off someone at their house. But apparently, she did not go straight home afterwards. Even though she only lived about 15 minutes or so away, Ebony did not arrive home in her driveway until about 4 a.m. To this day, she does not remember what transpired that night once she dropped that person off.

The only thing she could remember is stopping at a store called Junior's for a beer. One of Ebony's friend was there working behind the counter, but he would not sell her anything.

She walked outside and a guy who was in the store walked out behind her. He told Ebony he had something she could have. So, she followed him to a hotel where he was staying.

After pulling into the parking lot of the hotel, she must have blacked out. She remembers when she came to, she was getting in her vehicle and she then proceeded to peel out of the parking lot.

She was flying down a dark road driving over the speed limit when she was pulled over by the police. The officer got out of his patrol car and walked up to Ebony's car. He told her to stay in the vehicle. But she told him she needed to use the bathroom. She opened the car door and he stepped back to let her go behind the vehicle to relieve herself.

Suddenly a man with a dog on a leash, came out of nowhere. He yelled out to

Ebony, "Don't do that! Get back in the vehicle." She immediately raised up to give him a piece of her mind. Instantly he just disappeared. Then she went back around the vehicle and got in.

The police officer ask Ebony for her phone number. After writing it down, he then said, "Just go straight home, okay?" She responded with, "Yes sir" and drove off in one direction while he went in the other direction. The next thing she knew, she was standing outside of Corey's house, banging on his door. She has no recollection of his opening the door nor does she remember leaving his house.

She'd blacked out again. The next thing she recalled was pulling into her driveway where her husband was standing as he was about to get into his car. He helped her inside as she could barely stand up and proceeded to half carry her into the bathroom because she had urinated on herself.

Ebony had come face to face with the ups and downs she'd encountered in her childhood as well as her young adult life. She was left with the pain of it all without the passion to survive. In her mind there was only one thing left to do.

Her drinking had brought her to the brink of despair. It had reached its peak. Nothing mattered to her anymore. She came to the conclusion that she was a bad mother, wife, sister and daughter.

She knew the position she was in with her marriage, but couldn't seem to pull herself out of the depths of destruction. She just didn't know how. She felt like her kids would be better off without her. She knew she couldn't go on this way. That night, Ebony would attempt, for the last time, to take her life.

She can't remember all of the details, but with Ray's help, this is her account of what happened. In Ebony's drunken state, she got her husband's razor from the medicine cabinet and tried to cut her wrist. They struggled as he tried to take the razor from her. She ran into the kitchen and got a knife. Again, they struggled over the knife as well.

He would take one knife from her and she would grab another. In a drunken rage, they went back and forth this way until she passed out on the bed from shear exhaustion.

Thank God the kids did not wake up to see their mother this way. Ray said he was in shock! He'd never seen Ebony in such a bad state where she would constantly try to slit her wrist. He had no idea she was suicidal!

Later, Ray told Ebony he watched her throughout the night. He witnessed her speaking like a child in her sleep, a child being abused. He also witnessed her turn into another personality as she began to speak in another voice, a more comforting and soothing voice. The voice spoke out, "There, there now, don't blame yourself. It's not your fault. It was the doctor's fault." Then again, a change in personality back to the voice of a child, Ebony said, "I wish he were dead!"

For the first time Ray had observed the two personalities within one body. It was the body of his wife, Ebony. It was as though the child that needed to be protected, had never grown up and the child that took her place was the adult she had become. Ray would see his wife as she experienced unexplainable moaning and groaning escape her lips. He could not tell at times if she were awake or asleep. He said at times, her moaning sounded like she was in the heat of a passionate encounter with someone. At other times, she sounded as though she were being raped. Ebony would intermittently scream out and Ray kept trying to wake her up. She would open her eyes and look at him as if he were not her husband, but someone else. It was an emotionally and mentally rough night for Ebony, as well as an eye opening and shocking night for Ray.

The next morning, Ebony awoke, confused, tired, and drained. After her and Ray talked, they both came to the conclusion that Ebony should commit herself into a mental institution. That would turn out to be the best decision she could have made! Thank God! It turned out to be her way out of the dark place she was in.

CHAPTER 9

THE VICTORY OF RESTORATION

When Ebony woke up the next morning and realized what had happened, she knew she could no longer live this way. The devil had set a trap to destroy the plans God had for her. It was also a plan to take her out! She could not imagine what it would do to her children if they woke up one day and found Ebony dead. This was her second major attempt to kill herself! Her drinking was out of control. It had to stop! She hated MD for what he'd done to her. Yet she blamed herself for what she had become.

Over the years she had been told jokingly, by her family and her friends that she was an alcoholic. But Ebony was in denial. She believed once you acknowledged your weaknesses, you were responsible to do something to strengthen yourself in those areas and if you were not able to do it on your own, you were responsible to get help. So she would retort, "No I'm not! I can stop anytime I want to. I just don't want to!" Now her situation had become so daunting, that she knew it was time to own her failures. She had to admit she was an alcoholic, she was also broken, and she needed help to heal.

Ray told her that she was talking out of her head that night. She was also babbling on and on about how she wanted to kill someone.

She wondered, what if one day during one of her black out spells, she decided to go looking for the "Good Doctor?" Was she capable of murder during a black out?

Thank God they will never know. Yes, it was time to get help. Ebony had hit rock bottom. She knew she wasn't strong enough to stop drinking on her own, so, she told Ray she wanted to commit herself into a mental hospital. She had become a "suicidal alcoholic." She was tired of the struggle. She could no longer afford to worry or care about what people would think about her for committing herself to a mental hospital. After that night, she knew the alternative was much worse if she didn't commit herself.

Unknown to anyone, she had secretly been in counseling before this. It began as a scam to get drugs in order to increase her high. She had started going to a Christian Counseling Center and met with a nice female counselor named Mary Pouts. It would turn out that Mary was an angel sent from God. She talked to Ebony several times before referring her for a Psychiatric evaluation. This is what Ebony had hoped for. You see, she had been told if you were able to see a psychiatrist and you told him you were depressed, he would prescribe medication for the depression, which would also intensify the effects of alcohol.

However, she had not anticipated how much she would begin to enjoy just having someone to talk to who didn't blame her for everything that she was going through. She began feeling better about herself, even though she was still focused on getting drugs to enhance the alcohol. It helped her to escape the realities that haunted her every day.

Ebony was grateful for Miss Pouts because it was easier when it came down to committing herself into an institution on an inpatient basis. Because of her counseling sessions with Mary Pouts, she was ready. Ready to rise up and become the wife, mother, and woman, God had always intended for her to be!

God also had another angel in place in that hospital. The Lord was about to move in a mighty way in her life!

Ebony entered the hospital on a Friday. There were things her and the psychiatrist had talked about, which she refused to admit to herself. The things she dreaded most, had finally met her head on, face to face. There was no place to hide anymore. No place to run. The things she feared most were knocking at her door. It was a reality!

She had decided that her children deserved better than what she had been giving them. No child should ever have to utter the words,

"My mom was an alcoholic and committed suicide," or "My mom was never there for me."

Where Ebony came from, African Americans didn't normally talk about or address mental health issues. Nor did you see many people of their culture in mental hospitals. Illnesses of this type were generally frowned upon and therefore, they were swept under the rug, so to speak.

When people know you and have heard or witnessed some of your characteristics that show signs of instability or bizarre behavior patterns, they tend to keep their distance and tell others who don't know you, to keep theirs as well.

Part of Ebony's struggle was to admit to herself that she needed professional help in order to overcome her illness. She experienced so much pressure from the very people who, in one way or another played a role by their critical words that led to her low self-esteem. But God is good! Nobody had to tell her! She was finally able to take ownership of her actions and was now ready to admit to herself that she had a problem that was bigger than she was able to handle alone. Ebony was finally ready to do something about it. Some of you reading this book right now will say, "No, you can't be talking about the Ebony Richards I know, not the Sister Ebony that I know?"

These days, Ebony is filled with the joy of knowing, she may not be where she ought to be, but thanks be unto God, she is not where she used to be. We serve a God who is a restorer. "We serve a God who is a deliverer. We serve a God who is a redeemer." Ebony's life was never the same again.

After Ebony's 14 day stay in the hospital, she was finally released. Although it was not smooth sailing after that, she had at least taken the first step toward healing. Most importantly, she had given her heart to Christ.

It was a Friday morning that she was first admitted to the mental hospital. She was placed on a suicide watch. She was unresponsive, not eating, or speaking, or moving. She was monitored every 15 minutes. Ebony did a lot of crying those first few days. She wanted to get help but once she was admitted, the reality of her situation began to weigh her down.

There she was, alone, depressed, and suicidal. "Why me?" She asked herself. But God had a plan all along.

It was the weekend and there were no meetings, sessions, discussions, evaluations or anything of that nature conducted on the weekends. By Sunday night, Ebony felt the pangs of alcohol withdrawals attacking her body. She wanted a drink badly.

Instead of a drink, she ended up with a roommate. A woman was put in her room that Monday morning who was a Christian. She had been in this hospital twice before.

This was Ebony's first (and last) stay. Her new roommate began talking to her. But she really didn't feel like talking or being bothered with company. However, the woman was persistent. She talked and Ebony listened. Finally, on Tuesday, Ebony decided to talk to her.

By then the hospital had started giving her medication to help with the withdrawal symptoms, so she was beginning to feel better.

Ebony and her new roommate began to talk. She was curious to know why her roommate was there. She showed no signs of going through anything and she seemed very happy. She told Ebony she didn't know why she was there. She admitted herself for a rest as her children were irritating her and she needed to get away for a bit. She read her Bible all the time. She even shared scriptures with Ebony. How ironic that she would be placed in the room with Ebony who was a suicidal alcoholic! If you could ask Ebony today, she would tell you, her roommate was an angel sent from heaven. God put her there to minister to her heart.

Ebony began to follow her around and participate in whatever programs she participated in because they were spiritually based and she knew only God could deliver her out of the mess she was in. Her revelation was absolutely right!

One of the first things Ebony's roommate told her, was to have her family bring her a bible so she could read scriptures at the start and the finish of each day and so she did.

The first few days she was still depressed, and continued to be on suicide watch. It was very annoying because if she stayed in the shower too long, one of the nurses would knock on the door and ask if she were okay. If she didn't want to eat or talk to anyone, they were checking on her. The only reason Ebony talked to her roommate, was because she was a Christian lady who talked to her first.

After a few days, Ray bought her a bible and took it to her. Ebony began reading it every day. When her roommate talked to her about reading the Bible, once Ebony actually started reading it, she realized that this was new to her. She suggested that when Ebony got up in the morning, she should ask God to speak to her. Then close her eyes, open her Bible to a page, put her finger on the page, then open her eyes and read the scripture her finger pointed to.

To Ebony, this method of God speaking to her seemed a bit nonconventional, but she did as her roommate instructed. (Later she would learn a more organized method of reading her bible and she would come to understand that hearing from God was not limited to closing your eyes and putting your finger on a page. On the contrary! She would come to know that hearing from God would come more frequently as she continually kept her ears in a posture of inclination and always developed her relationship with Him daily through prayer, and reading His word).

Every morning, Ebony would wake up and open her bible to a scripture. Her roommate would also tell her to look in the mirror and to speak words of affirmation and speak God's promises out loud as she read. Ebony would get up in the morning and open her bible to a scripture and speak it out loud as her roommate told her to do, even though she felt a little silly doing it.

But God! My God! Jehovah Rapha! On the eighth day (8 means new beginnings) October 31, 1993, Ebony would have the visit of a lifetime. It was not painful, but passionate. It was a visit from God. That morning started off as usual. She opened her Bible to pick a scripture at random to meditate on. That scripture was from the book of Psalms 61:1- 4. It says, "Hear my cry O God; attend unto my prayer. From the end of the earth will I cry unto thee, when my heart is overwhelmed: lead me to the rock that is higher than I. For thou hast been a shelter for me and a strong tower from the enemy. I will abide in thy tabernacle forever: I will trust in the covert of thy wings."

As she read this scripture over and over, something began to happen. She felt tingly all over and the room grew dim except for certain spots. She began to dance and shout. She has been sober and walking with the

Lord from that time on. You see, the enemy thought that she was going to be his by his birthday. But God chose to visit her and save her on Halloween, to show Satan that he was a liar and a defeated foe. The book of 1 John 4:4 (KJV) says: "Ye are of God little children and have overcome them: because greater is He that is in you, than he that is in the world."

Ebony has not even thought about backsliding. God restored her life in that room, on that day. She became whole on that day for God's purpose. The healing didn't happen overnight, but little by little as Ebony stayed close to God and began to abide in his word, God took away her pain and exchanged if for passion. He took away her ashes and gave her beauty in their place, her beauty.

One of the scriptures that would always bless Ebony came from, I John 5:4 (KJV), "For whatsoever is born of God overcometh the world: and this is the victory that overcometh the world."

The Lord restored the years that the canker worm had stolen. She was no longer an ugly duckling. Whenever she returns to her hometown for a visit, people that knew her before, do a double take when they see her now. They can't believe their eyes. They ask what she is doing and how is she able to look so radiant. She tells them it is the glory of the Lord.

In the book of Eccl. 3:11 (KJV), it says, "He hath made everything beautiful in his time: also he hath set the world in their heart, so that no man can find out the work that God maketh from the beginning to the end.

It was only by God's grace that Ebony came through this, so that she could help someone else. God not only restored her passion for life, but He gave her a passion for others. He gave her a passion for the things He is passionate about.

One of the things she is passionate about, is her love for Israel and the people of Israel. She knows that this passion could only be put there by God.

Psalm 122 (KJV) says, "I was glad when they said unto me, Let us go into the house of the Lord. Our feet shall stand within thy gates, O Jerusalem. Jerusalem is builded as a city that is compact together: Whither the tribes go up, the tribes of the Lord, unto the testimony of Israel, to give thanks unto the name of the Lord. For there are set thrones of judgment, the thrones of the house of David. Pray for the peace of Jerusalem: they shall prosper that love thee. Peace be within thy walls, and prosperity within thy palaces. For my brethren and companions' sakes, I will now say, peace be within thee. Because of the house of the Lord our God I will seek thy good. Ebony gives Him all the glory."

He did not have to do it. But He did. Not only did He give her a heart of passion, He let her know that part of her healing would be contingent upon her forgiveness for the individual who abused her. Now that was hard, really hard. There is no way to pretend.

It would take Ebony some time to truly and totally forgive "MD." Nevertheless, with

God as her help, she was able to forgive, even though he never acknowledged, nor did he ever apologize for his actions, prior to his death. Ebony knows that forgiveness is for her, not him.

"Forgiveness is very important to God. It is so important, that if we choose not to forgive, He chooses not to forgive us. If we don't, He won't! It is as simple as that!"

CHAPTER 10

JESUS IS THE ANSWER

If you are reading this book, and you, or someone you know has been abused, or is being abused, don't feel that you are alone. The devil wants us to think that we are crazy and if we tell anybody, they will think we are crazy also. But that is simply not true. Besides, even if they do...so what? Just know that Jesus can do all things. But you must be a part of His family. So, if you are, great! If you are not, let's start your healing process today by opening your heart to God. Accept Jesus as your Lord and Savior today. Romans 10:9-10 (KJV). That if thou shalt confess with thy mouth the Lord Jesus, and shalt believe in thine heart that God hath raised him from the dead, thou shall be saved. For with the heart man believeth unto righteousness; and with the mouth confession is made unto salvation.

Now, if you are ready to accept the Lord Jesus Christ in your heart, just pray this prayer and let Him begin to heal you.

Lord, I pray that you would come into my life today. I choose to believe in my heart and I confess with my mouth, according to Romans 10:9-10, that Jesus died on the cross for my sins. He was raised three days later with all power. I'm asking you to be my Lord and my Savior. I trust you and I want to be yours forever. Thank you for saving me. In Jesus name I pray. Amen

If you prayed that prayer, you now belong to the family of God. You are a new creation in Christ Jesus. Now find a local church and begin to get Godly council. They can help you to find the best council for your needs. Don't be afraid! Do it today! Tomorrow is not promised.

Ebony's Prayer for you:

"Lord, I first want to thank you for being God. You sent your son to be the example of pain and passion and Lord, I thank you for the one who is reading this book right now. The one who has accepted you as Lord and Savior over their life. I pray that you would make them whole. I pray that today they would give their life to you if they are not saved so they would know that there is hope in Jesus. Heal their heart Lord. Turn their pain into passion just as you did for me, so that they may help someone else to be healed. Lord, I thank you for their salvation and their healing. In Jesus name I pray, Amen!

CHAPTER 11

POEMS/SONGS FROM THE CRIES OF A CHILD

These poems were written by Ebony to help her in her healing process. By putting her feelings in writing and releasing them, they helped her to cope during her times of struggle.

The Pain (POEM)

Tears built up, falling in instead of out

Can't let no one know what my pain is about

Just an ugly duckling to pick on …you see

But I understand… I don't even want to be me

Been through so much over the years

But I got to be strong and hold back the tears

Feel like a sponge, got all I can hold

But cannot cry out, the secret can't be told

May hurt my family, or friends of theirs you see

So, I got to hold back. Besides, they won't believe me

But one day I know, one day soon

The pain will be gone the passion will resume

Searching (POEM)

I had a void I wanted to fill

I tried alcohol and every kind of pill

Nothing I tried worked for long

Right wasn't working, so I searched wrong

Things got worse by day and by night

I wanted to give up and forfeit my right

But one day while in the midst of the fight

Jesus stepped in and shined a light

I placed you in this world

And only I can take you out

Don't give up BELOVED

A change is coming about

Do as he Says (POEM)

Alone in a room, sitting undressed on a table

Afraid to call out for help. Don't know God is able

For where is He? If He could only tell my mother

"Go check on your baby girl, before he hurts her"

Though my screams are silent. The pain is unbearable

But it's just a checkup. I can't become hysterical

For what do I know, I'm only four

He's an adult. He says undress and close the door

So, I do as he says out of obedience to my mother

Listen to the doctor. Respect your elder

He won't hurt you. He's here to make you better

She says please do as he says, as they both leave together

He comes back alone. She seldom comes in

Never asks what he does. She calls him our friend

He touches me in places, you wouldn't dream of

Why does she say he shows me much love

But he is the doctor and he knows best

So, I do as mom says when it's time to undress

The check-ups are frequent. Painful in many ways

But again, mom just tells me, to do as he says

I'm being obedient mom. But I don't understand

It's so painful to me. What he does with his hand

He says I'm a good girl. Gives me money as well

Says this is our little secret, so I'm afraid to tell

I'm being good mom. On this table I lay

I am being obedient. I do as you say

God please get my mommy

I can't breathe with this in my mouth

He says I'm a good girl

But what's this about

It makes me gag…I just threw up

He laughed and said "you're growing up

Can't move my lips. But my mind prays

God sent my angel to do as he says

I am asleep now, flying through the air

I'm a beautiful angel. No one can hurt me there

Look there's Jesus! He calls me near

Says don't worry. And have no fear

For one day this pain will be replaced

With love and passion toward the human race

Beauty for ashes if you follow my way

One day you will wake up and do as I say

When I'm at your feet, I soar high (SONG)

I think of all the times that you lifted me

high above my problems and set me free

Lord I know you have a plan

That includes every woman and every man

But it's hard to see you using me

After all I've been put through

Lord were you there at the bed

When as a child, I lay naked and afraid

Can't ever remember experiencing such pain

Just wanted my mommy to never bring me again

But as we turned and walked away

The good doctor stood up

And with a smile, he hugged me and said

See you next month for another check up

I'm eleven now and still a monthly visit I get

Maybe this is normal or maybe soon it will quit

Lord can you hear my cry

Take me out of this before I die

Lord please keep me at your feet

I feel that nothing can hurt me there

I soar like the angels

Flying high above in the air

I think of all the times that you lifted me

high above my problems and set me free

Lord I know you have a plan

That includes every woman, and every man

But it's hard to see you using me

After all I've put so many through

I think of all the things I used to do

My marriage, my family, and myself

I almost destroyed it all. But you never let me fall

And when the pain I could not stand

And stood with a knife in my hand

Lord you stepped into the fight

Took over the struggle of the night

And lifted me high upon a rock

Said it's not your time by my clock

You put me back into the race

But now at a different pace

You showed me how to sit at your feet

Where there is never any defeat

So, Lord I thank you for a new high

Without sin, guilt, or shame, it comes at your

feet and will always be my aim

//The End//

BIOGRAPHY

Ethel T. Washington, (AKA, Ethel Tippit) is a native of Cottonport, Louisiana. She was born in the 60's to Lawrence and Dora Tippit. After a life of struggles with alcohol, she was introduced to the Lord in a profound way. At the age of 30, she gave her life to Christ and began her walk with the Lord in Panama City Florida in October 1993. In 1997, she moved to Okinawa, Japan with her (former) husband and 3 children.

In 1998, after a 40-day church fast, she received her call to ministry, as an Evangelist, under Apostles Thomas and Phyllis Terry, at God's Way Love Center in Okinawa. Evangelist Washington has also been called to minister in dance as a prophetic dancer, ministering in liturgical praise, worship and ministry of mime. In July 2012, Evangelist Washington was ordained as a Minister and Elder at New Dimensions Ministries. In December 2015, she was installed as an Elder at Clarion Call Christian Center, where she is now an active member, serving as a licensed and ordained Evangelist and Elder, teaching, preaching and ministering in the dance.

61487949R00065

Made in the USA
Columbia, SC
23 June 2019